Captivating

HEART TO HEART

FACILITATOR'S GUIDE

OTHER BOOKS BY JOHN AND STASI ELDREDGE

Captivating: Unveiling the Mystery of a Woman's Soul

Captivating Study Guide

Captivating: A Guided Journal

Captivating

HEART TO HEART

FACILITATOR'S GUIDE

STASI ELDREDGE

THOMAS NELSON
Since 1798

NASHVILLE DALLAS MEXICO CITY RIO DE JANEIRO BEIJING

Published in Nashville, Tennessee. Thomas Nelson is a trademark of Thomas Nelson, Inc.

Thomas Nelson, Inc., titles may be purchased in bulk for educational, business, fund-raising, or sales promotional use. For information, please e-mail SpecialMarkets@ThomasNelson.com.

Published in association with Yates & Yates, LLP, Attorneys and Counselors, Orange, California.

Unless otherwise noted, all Scripture quotations are taken from *The Holy Bible,* NEW INTERNATIONAL VERSION®. NIV®. Copyright©1973, 1978, 1984 by International Bible Society. Used by permission of Zondervan. All rights reserved.

Additional Scripture quotations are taken from the following source:
(NASB) New American Standard Bible, © 1960, 1977 by the Lockman Foundation.

Facilitator's Guide: Captivating Heart to Heart
ISBN: 1-4185-2755-6

ISBN-13: 978-1-4185-2755-6

Printed in the United States of America

07 08 09 10 11 WOR 5 4 3 2 1

Contents

Introduction

G od is on the move. The beavers say it in *The Chronicles of Narnia* as "Aslan is on the move," with holy and hushed expectation. We can say it the same way. God *loves* his church, the Bride of Christ, more than most of us have yet grasped. And He loves each one of us personally, intimately. Always has. Always will. This series embraces that truth and because of His love, invites women to get to know Jesus better; to come closer; to look at their lives through his eyes and to receive the healing, the comfort, the embrace, the encouragement, the dignity and the calling that he longs to bestow upon each one of us.

Powerful things, life-changing things happen to women when they encounter Jesus in a personal way. The unique way that God has been moving in women's lives as told through the messages in *Captivating* is nothing short of breathtaking and beautiful. Miraculous really.

Now you may not feel up to the task of leading women through this. That's okay. Neither do I! The good news is, you don't have to have any experience leading women to take a few gals with you on this journey. With God's help, we've created a tool in this DVD series that God will use to set *women free*. All you need to do is invite them in, provide a place for this to happen and share your own journey as a fellow pilgrim. We'll show you how to use this tool in this Facilitator's Guide. All you need to do is take the plunge and God will take care of the rest.

How to Use This Tool

LEADING IN A CHURCH SETTING

First off, thank you. Thank you for following God's call and choosing to do this and for making it available to the women in your church. I have so many, many stories of God coming in new and mighty ways for women through *Captivating*, and I am excited about what he will be doing in you and in the women of your church. God loves to come for us. He will continue to come!

Have fun with this series! Have an absolute blast! Partnering with God for the purposes of bringing healing and freedom to be His Bride is just the best way to be spending your life.

But I must caution you. This is no ordinary, powerful biblical study. This is big-time serious, front lines stuff. You want to be certain that God has called you to bring this now and when you are, don't do this alone. It is imperative that you have your church leadership's support. It is also essential that you have people praying for you throughout the duration of the study. Ask a handful of friends near and far to intercede for you! If you expect a large number of women to attend, you will want to recruit small group leaders to assist you. (You will be breaking up into small groups of about six to ten women each.) The ladies you gather will be leading the small groups, and you will be leading them. You also can lead a small group yourself. Together, you will work and pray as a team.

Small group leaders need to read (or re-read) the entire book *Captivating* prior to meeting and go through as much of the study guide as possible before your group begins. About a week before you begin, it's a good idea if you can gather the leadership team *at least once* to pray and talk through the flow of the study. Encourage these women to ask friends to pray for them as well! As soon as you have the names of the women coming to the study allocated into small groups, give their names to their group leaders so they can begin to pray for them. A good prayer is a simple one . . . *that God will accomplish all he desires in each woman throughout the study; that God reign in every aspect and that the women come to know Jesus more truly and deeply.* That's the goal, pure and simple. And you can rest in knowing that God will answer this prayer . . . and more profoundly than you can imagine!

Logistically, you will need to make arrangements for

+ a large gathering room

+ smaller, private rooms for the small groups to meet in

+ a DVD player and screen—large enough for all the women to see and hear and of a high quality so it plays well and cleanly (VERY IMPORTANT!)

+ a CD player

A WORD ABOUT SMALL GROUPS

Let's talk about small group dynamics for a moment. Women will be entering in on any given day with a variety of issues and concerns pulling at their hearts and minds. That is one reason why it is so very important to begin each time with prayer. Invite the Holy Spirit to guide and reign in your time together and allow the women the time to silently lay all their concerns at Jesus' feet. Then they are not distracted from receiving what the Lord has for them on *that* particular day. Begin the formal portion of every small group this way. Don't make it a long prayer. Just short and sweet and there you are.

OK. By the very nature of the material being talked about, it is important that you keep your group size small. Twelve women is too large. Ten is the maximum. Two the minimum. If your group expands to fifteen women or so because you don't want to turn anyone away, *the entire group experience will be dramatically compromised.* Keep it small. Pray for more group leaders if the need arises, and pray that the women God wants in the group at this particular time are the ones in it. You can trust God to come for those women not able to join the group due to size constraints. He will. He really will.

Women will be coming in nervous, excited, hopeful, *and* scared when you first begin to gather. Most will not be willing to immediately share from their hearts and lives while others will be ready to dominate the group with their own stories! Navigating the hearts of the women while you guide the direction of the time will require the guidance of the Holy Spirit. As the facilitator of the small group, your personal walk and dependence upon God are of the utmost importance. Leading this will cause you to grow! But you can rest in knowing that God cares beyond measure about each woman, about you, and you can trust Him to help you lead!

Women like to talk. Naturally. We have a lot of important things to say. Gently "shutting down" a woman when she is taking the group in the wrong direction or overly dominating the group's time can be done graciously. Say something along the lines of, "That's a very important matter, Mary. I wish that we had the time to discuss that at length here but unfortunately, we don't." You can offer to talk privately with her or for her to bring the issue up again at the end of your time and invite those who are able to stay to do so. You probably won't have to. You may want to. Let the Holy Spirit guide you.

You will have brokenhearted women in your group. You can count on that because we are *all* brokenhearted. Actually, one of the key goals of the group is for the healing of Christ to come for the women. But you may have a woman that is broken incredibly deeply and is only now beginning to turn with hope to Jesus for the possibility of healing. The session on the Wound will be especially difficult (but good) for her. If you find that each small group time is turning into a group therapy session solely for this one woman, you will want to speak with her privately and recommend counseling to her. Before you do, ask your church and others you trust for a good, Christian counselor to recommend her to.

Some women may not be as interested in learning together as in making a doctrinal point. You will need to shut that down as well. Saying something like, "You know, Frances, this isn't the right format to hold a doctrinal debate. I respect your convictions and I ask you to respect mine (ours) as well. Today, we're focusing on (whatever the topic is) and I'm going to have to end this so we can get back on track." You can be firm and kind at the same time. Chances are, this won't happen . . . but it may!

On the other hand, and this is *very* important, there will be times when a woman is sharing something honest and painful from her life and the temptation will be to offer her quick advice and platitudes. For example, in one small group I was a part of, there was a young woman who shared about the crisis her marriage was in . . . her husband abandoning the Lord, the children, etc. The group was young and we did not know the woman well or anything about her life beyond what she had shared that day.

Women were quick with advice and empty encouragement. They offered her promises from Scripture that felt like Band-aids on a hemorrhaging heart. The effect of their well-meaning words was to shut this woman's heart down and prevent her from sharing honestly painful things in the future. It was very sad. And I have seen it/heard it done countless times.

And this will be very hard *not* to do. We don't like it when others are hurting. We don't want to leave them in it or feel powerless to help. We want to help. The way to help in your small group is to listen, to empathize, to acknowledge the woman's legitimate sorrow and let her feel heard and understood. There may be a time for godly advice and counsel. Offering promises from Scripture is wonderful . . . when done with the right motivation. Praying for her at the end of your time or perhaps at the end of her sharing is absolutely valid.

You will need to coach the group on this before you begin; teaching and guiding them throughout your gatherings.

Make a covenant of confidentiality. What is shared in the group stays in the group. This is of the utmost importance so that women feel safe enough to share from their lives.

YOUR PART

At your very first gathering, you will need to give the women the "ground rules." I would do this about ¾ into your introduction. They need the information, but do not want it to feel like they are in elementary school with a list of do's and don'ts. After giving them some "housekeeping" details, go back and recap the gist of your introduction.

Housekeeping: Cell phones need to be turned off. If they are unable to do that, then they must set them on silent and quietly and as unobtrusively as possible leave the room should they need to take a call.

Women need to know where the bathrooms are!

They need to know the flow of the time. Here is what we suggest:

They arrive. If there is childcare available, then they will need to allow plenty of time to safely and happily arrange their children. In a large church setting, this could take as long as 15 minutes. Therefore, your first session will probably start a little late as women figure out the logistics.

Are you going to have beverages and snacks available? Do you want to do a sign-up sheet? Though not necessary, most women enjoy having something available and if it's in the morning, this may be their first opportunity to have a little snack. But it should be simple.

Allow time for women to get situated, seated, greet their friends, and meet new people. If the group is small and meeting in your home, introduce the women to each other. Invite them to have something to drink/eat. Tell them that you will be starting in however many minutes.

If your group is large, have your small group facilitators ready and available to greet and welcome the women; to introduce themselves and invite them to have something to eat/drink. The more personal the greeting, the better! The small group leaders will be a tremendous help in inviting the women to sit down so you may begin on time.

Once you all sit down, you will be talking to/teaching them, watching the DVD together, and then having a five-minute journaling time. This will take about an hour. Then you will be having a 5- to 10-minute break.

After the break, the women will be re-gathering together to go through the study guide. In a church setting, they will be breaking up into small groups—as many as are necessary. The women will need to know whose group they are in and where they will be meeting. This can be done either before the first meeting, by phone, at the break or at the beginning of your first gathering. Either way, it will take the women a few extra minutes this first time to get situated.

You will be meeting in your small groups for about 45 minutes. The time will fly by. You will not possibly be able to answer every question or even allow for every woman to share at *every* gathering. I have given suggested directions for each of the specific lessons. Of course, they are merely *suggestions*. You are free to follow the Holy Spirit wherever He leads!

Leading in a Home

Much of the information about leading this series in a church applies to those of you who are leading this series in a home. But you have an advantage because the intimacy of this series lends itself well to the comforts, privacy and coziness of a home.

You will need to be in a place free from interruption. If others are home, they have to know . . . "Don't come in!" unless it's an emergency. You will need a CD player, a DVD player, and about an additional two hours each week to prepare and to pray. Part of that time is previewing the DVD for the week in order to be better prepared for where we are going.

The primary way you facilitate this series is by example. By leading, you are *not* saying that you have it all mastered and perfectly understood! No, you are only saying, I am going on this journey. I believe Christ has more for us here, through this series and as a fellow pilgrim, I'm inviting you to join me. Your own desires and vulnerability are what will have the greatest impact on the group. Walk with God! Have a few friends outside of your group commit to be praying for you!

You will be learning much as you lead. Know that this study is as much for you as for anyone else and that God is so pleased with your courage and your desire to go further with him!

Read about Small Group Dynamics. Read through the first lesson of this guide which explains each step. Take a deep breath. Pray. And then, have an absolute blast! This is going to be awesome.

The Heart of a Woman

OPENING

W e've found that a very powerful way to reach women is to use film clips they are familiar with; movies they love. Better still are the trailers from those films. The trailers tell the story, in a powerful way, in about three minutes. These stories and visual contexts act as "short cuts to the heart." The trailers are created for all audiences and therefore won't have any potentially offensive language or situations in them. (You will, of course, want to pre-screen everything you choose to show.) For the opening time of your very first gathering, begin by showing the trailer to *Braveheart* (Trailer 2). I use it, along with *Anna and the King*, and *The Chronicles of Narnia* at the retreats we lead. And I do mean, start with it. No introduction. Dim the lights and play the trailer(s). This has two powerful effects. For one, women love them. It captures their attention and their hearts, and two, it lets them know right off, that this is going to be different than church group gatherings they've been in before.

(By the way, you don't have to use the film clips to make this a powerful experience. The DVD series itself will do that. But from years of leading groups and retreats for women, I can tell you that the clips are a really good addition. The theatrical trailers for a film are usually available on the commercial DVDs, and are also valuable tools to introduce the overall themes of a movie. You are going to need all of the equipment necessary to show the Heart to Heart series anyway so you might as well go for it!)

THE GOAL FOR LESSON ONE

The goal for this lesson is simply to *awaken the women's hearts* and, further, to awaken them to the truth that their hearts *matter*. As women, they possess and share core desires—desires that express themselves uniquely but *are there*.

We want to awaken their memory of their childhood and hopefully to a time of wonder and endless possibilities. What were their dreams?

We want to awaken them to the desires they possess today. This may take some time. Perhaps a better way to say it is that we want them to awaken to the possibility that they still do have core desires, ones that are good, placed there by God and a part of their glory.

Ultimately, and throughout the series, we want to restore dignity to their feminine hearts, to femininity itself.

YOUR INTRODUCTION

Once the trailer is finished, bring up the lights. I usually begin by reacting to the trailer . . . say what it stirs in me! That it reminds me of what I most deeply long for as a woman—to be romanced, to play an irreplaceable role in a heroic adventure, and to be the beauty of a great story. Then welcome the women! Share your excitement and delight that they are here. Set the stage for your time together by laying out a vision. Here's why we're getting together, here is how many weeks we'll meet, for how long each week. Tell them that it's a ten-part series, that your plan is to watch one part each week, do some work in the study guide prior to coming, break and talk about it. Most important, tell them your desire for them, why you've called them together. Tell them what's on your heart.

Give them the ground rules.

IMPORTANT:

The Captivating: Heart to Heart DVD *series does not follow exactly the flow of the book* Captivating. *There are twelve chapters in the book but only ten lessons on the DVD. Some lessons in the DVD series and study guide involve reading two chapters in the book rather than one, but not necessarily consecutive chapters! Because of this, it is helpful if all the participants read through the entire book before beginning the study (even if it's just a quick, light read).*

If you want to set the tone by playing a particular song—one that would access their heart in a way that compliments the lesson, this would be the time to do it.

Think of this entire lesson as the *Introduction*. An introduction to their heart, if you will.

If you are going to pray in front of the women, pray a simple prayer inviting Jesus to come. Nothing long. Just something heartfelt and brief.

WATCH THE VIDEO

It will help prepare you to preview the video before your group meets. Some are a little longer than others, and you may need to edit them to fit your schedule if you have time constraints.

QUIET REFLECTION

At the end of each session that you watch, get back in front of the women and give them three to five minutes to journal their thoughts and reactions to what they have just watched. What did it stir in them? What would they like to ask? Play some soft, beautiful background music during this time. Soundtracks from films are a good choice. The soundtracks to *A River Runs Through It, Braveheart, Titanic, The Mission* and *Pearl Harbor* are some good ones.

BREAK

At the end of the journaling time, invite the women to take a break. As this is your first gathering, you will need to give more specific instructions. The women need to know what is available and where. They also need to know how long the break is going to be. Women will generally take longer than you give them. If you begin when you say you will, however, they will quickly learn to confine themselves to the time allowed.

IN A HOME

It's nice to have some small snack available, but it is not necessary. Have it available as the women arrive and mingle before the "official" group time begins. At the break, they can help themselves to a fresh cup of coffee or some fruit or whatever before settling back down again. Depending on the size of the group, the break should be anywhere from five to ten minutes, allowing them plenty of time to use the facilities and check for messages on their phones if need be.

SHARE: HEART TO HEART

OK. This is going to be the most powerful part of the experience—processing what they are discovering. The questions I recommend are only a guide. Trust your instincts. Walk with God. If you feel you want to head in another direction, go for it! Before I suggest the questions to run with, let me offer some additional advice on facilitating small groups.

+ Start with less personal questions. The women may not know each other well yet and may not feel comfortable right off the bat sharing about their lives, dreams and desires. Help them get used to small group discussion by leading off each session with an easier-to-answer question. Then progressively move to the harder issues.

+ Lead by example. This is a very personal journey. When it comes to the more sensitive questions, I suggest you be ready to go first. Don't dominate the time but let your vulnerability create a safe place for theirs.

+ Stay focused. You can't possibly cover all the material from the study guide during your discussion time. Pick a handful of questions and stay focused on them. I'll make recommendations for each week. You may not even get through the questions I recommend, but you certainly won't if you let the conversation wander. Keep it on track with a kind but firm direction.

+ Ground Rules: I think it's important to lay down a couple of ground rules for small groups the very first time you gather. Don't be heavy and don't come down on them or make it sound legalistic. Just state a few simple rules. (1) *Confidentiality.* Every woman agrees that nothing gets passed along outside the group. What's shared in the group stays in the group. Break this rule and you will no longer be welcome. (2) *No teaching.* There are many gifted women and some of them will be tempted to take the stand and begin teaching the others. Make it clear that we're here to listen and ask questions. (3) Respect the women. *Try not to "fix" each other or offer advice.* As a woman shares her story, listen well. Ask questions. Affirm her. But don't tell her how to live her life. Don't offer advice *unless she asks for it.*

OK. Now for the discussion questions of Lesson One.

QUESTIONS

1. As the heart is central, begin by having a few women read Proverbs 4:23 from a few different translations of the Bible. What does it mean? Guide them from the "watch over your heart" like a guard dog understanding to the truth of "*caring for your heart.*"

2. Invite every woman to share some of her favorite movies or books. Facilitators may go first to pave the way. After every woman has had a chance to speak, point out that most all of the movies they talked about have one or more of the core desires of a woman's heart: to be romanced, to be irreplaceable, and to unveil beauty. Help them to make the connection.

Not all women will have romance movies as their favorites; some will have action or war movies. Those speak to our desires as well—to play an irreplaceable role and also, as in *Braveheart,* to be the inspiration to a man like William Wallace.

1. Ask the women who they want *to be* in those stories/movies. Let this linger a while. Why do they want to be this person? This isn't to embarrass the women but to let their hearts begin to rise to the surface. As the facilitator, it's a good idea to write this down for every woman as it will give you great insight into her. Remembering this will come in handy for later discussions.

2. Now go back into their childhood. What were the games they loved to play as little girls? Use the video as an example. Cherie loved to dress up in a turquoise sequined tutu with a wand. Lori loved to tap dance on the stage (her parents' entryway) and later so did her daughters. What did they love to do?

3. Bring it back to Scripture. Read Genesis 1:26. We are made in the image of God. "In the image of God, he created him . . . *male and female* he created them." Where do we bear the image of God? In our feminine hearts. Transition into sharing about our core desires. It is in our desires that we bear the image of God . . . therefore, they are not meant to be a source of shame, contempt or embarrassment . . . but a source of great dignity.

4. How did they define the desire to be romanced? This needs to be fleshed out and made to go beyond the scope of candlelight dinners. The desire is expansive—to be wanted, pursued, desired as a woman . . . to be seen and enjoyed.

5. How do they feel about having this desire? What are they doing with it?

6. Remind them that God longs to be desired, wanted and pursued as well. He says, "You will seek me and find me when you seek me with all your heart" (Jeremiah 29:13).

7. Back to their childhood or teen years, what were the dreams they held for themselves when they were young? What did they want to be or do? Another way to get at this is by asking again about the movies or characters they would love to be. In the DVD, Julie talked about Eowyn . . . her fierceness, her courage, her dignity and her tenderness. She wants to be irreplaceable like that. (From the Scriptures, you can talk about Esther or Mary, the mother of Jesus, as two prime examples of women who played their irreplaceable role well and changed the world for tremendous life.)

8. It takes great courage to play the role that is ours to play. It also takes great vulnerability that flows from trusting the heart of God. Allowing them to dream . . . if they could be or do anything now, what would it be?

9. Again, bring the women back to the great dignity of this desire to play an irreplaceable role in a heroic adventure because this desire is given to us by God and where/how we bear his image. Our Lord desires to be irreplaceable to us!

10. Beauty. Beauty is tied deeply to our irreplaceable role. We will be talking of this more later, but what do the women do with this word? Do they own the desire to be beautiful?

Now this is key. The desire to be beautiful, to have a beauty all our own to unveil is not primarily about our looks. It is a desire to be captivating in the depths of *who you are*.

11. We want them to begin to see that: 1) the desire for a beauty to unveil is much deeper than their outward appearance but flows from an inward beauty, and 2) that because they are made in the image of God, they do possess it. This may not come until later. For now, ask the question, "Who is beautiful to you and why?" This will help to flesh out the broader definition. We will be going into much greater detail with this and with the other core desires as well. Remember, today is merely *Introduction*.

12. Read Psalm 27:4. God is beautiful. His creation is beautiful. He wants to be worshipped as beautiful for who he is and for what he has done. It is a holy desire.

13. All women are living to varying degrees with unmet desires. What are they doing with the ache of their unmet desires?

WRAP-UP

God is inviting us as women to trust Him with our desires. To allow him to awaken us more deeply, to restore them to us, and even to deepen them. The desires he placed in our hearts as women are not there to torment us but to speak to us of what is true; who we really are and the role that is ours to play. God wants us not to deaden our hearts but to bring our aching hearts to him. There is life ahead. There is substantial healing ahead. There is romance and beauty and meaning ahead. All to be found in the love of God. Our hearts matter . . . to our God!

Pray and entrust the women's hearts to God. This is a sample prayer from *Captivating: A Guided Journal*:

> *Dear Jesus,*
>
> *I love you. I need you. I come before you now, once again, as yours, asking for your help, your grace. My life is yours. My heart is yours. Would you please come and shine your light into the depths of my heart that I might understand myself better and come to know your healing and your presence more deeply? Help me to remember what I need to remember. Help me to see, to understand, to repent, to forgive, and to become. Jesus, I give you access to all of my heart. I invite you into every part. Come, Holy Spirit, have your way . . . that I might love you, God, more deeply and truly with all of my heart, soul, mind and strength.*
>
> *In Jesus' name I pray.*
> *Amen.*

Created Eve / Fallen Eve

The Goal

The goal of lesson two is to further reveal and enjoy the wonder and beauty of Eve's creation and to begin to restore the dignity of her being Adam's "helper-completer" . . . his *ezer*. (We will go into having an irreplaceable role more deeply in the last lesson.)

We also want the women to *begin* to grasp the vast implications of bearing the image of God—with Beauty being the "essence" of femininity, and the life-giving power of beauty.

Sadly, we have to turn to the "Fall" all too quickly. But within the context of God's mercy and our "sisterhood" if you will, we will explore that fallenness is common ground to all women. We want to unveil the tragedy of the Fall and the implications on their lives; to uncover the way(s) that they in particular tend to sin.

And then invite them to continue to repent and receive God's forgiveness and healing.

Your Introduction

I'd begin week two by welcoming the women back and setting up your time together by saying something like, "This week may be a little harder. This week we are going to take a look at the ways we tend to act out of our fallenness. We all have fallen. We all still struggle with our flesh. And as women, we tend to sin along the spectrum of being controlling and driven to being desolate and needy. And in a variety of ways, underneath it all, we are *hiding*. I'm going to show you a pretty funny scene from the movie *My Big Fat Greek Wedding* that shows a woman *hiding*." (Scene 2; 10:40—15:30) Be sure to watch the scene/movie first so that you can set it up appropriately and time it. The suggested scene begins in the restaurant early in the movie where Tulah's family is discussing her future. She overhears them and later goes outside. Tulah is hiding behind outdated clothes and glasses. She is hiding her desires by living and working as she believes her family wants her to and trying to kill the desires of her heart. And finally, she is hiding behind a counter. End the scene after the man pays her.

I would then say something like, "It's a funny scene. But there isn't anything funny about the cost born to others when we hide . . . when we withhold who we are and do not offer our true selves."

You may want to play a song here to quiet their hearts or simply watch the video. Suggested Song: "Arms of Mercy," Kim Hill (*Arms of Mercy*)

WATCH THE VIDEO

QUIET REFLECTION

Say, "I'm going to play some music for a few minutes before our break now, and while I do, I want you to journal your thoughts and reactions to the DVD. What did it stir in you? What do you want to bring to God?"

BREAK

SHARE; HEART TO HEART

At the start of your small group time, I'd remind the women of the ground rules. "Hey gals, just a reminder . . ." You won't need to do this, of course, it you are meeting with a group of women you know well and trust. But new groups may need a reminder as they learn how to be together.

1. God said in Genesis 2:18 that it was not good for man to be alone. Why not? And how important does that make Eve?

2. Kind of like the story of our creation itself, we don't linger long in the DVD talking about the glory of Eve's creation. But before we leave the garden, talk a bit about the progression of creation. What does their heart do with us referring to Eve as the "crown of creation"? Did they believe that since Eve was created second, she came in second place to the heart and love of God?

3. Talk a little bit about the many ways that Eve bears the image of God (tender, merciful, inviting, fierce, fiercely devoted, and beautiful). What are some favorite aspects of the power of beauty we talked about in Chapter Two of *Captivating*?

4. Read Genesis 3:6. Why did Eve eat the forbidden fruit? (The answers you are going for are along the lines of . . . "She did not trust the heart of God. She believed he was holding out on her. She did not believe his heart toward her was good." This is where we see we are all daughters of Eve. To varying degrees, *we still believe this*.)

5. The women will be quick to identify what is most deeply marred in men after the Fall is their essence; *strength*. Their fallen nature expresses itself on the spectrum from weak and passive to violent and abusive. It is a harder jump for women to see that their essence is beauty and that when woman fell, what became most deeply marred was her tender vulnerability, her mercy. Do they understand this?

6. On the Fallen Eve spectrum of controlling/dominating to mousy and desolate, which ways did their mothers (and/or the influential women in their lives growing up) tend to sin? Ask for examples.

7. OK. We are all in the same boat here. We have all fallen. We are all being sanctified and healed, but none of us are perfect yet! Within the context of confidentiality and shared weakness, have the women share. Which way do they tend to go (controlling vs. desolate) and how does it play out in their lives?

8. What about indulging? Are they aware that there are things they may be doing to numb the ache in their hearts?

9. Hiding? In the DVD, we talk about hiding in business, distraction, daydreaming, silence, shame, and not offering.

Read Genesis 3:10. Underneath all our hiding is a deep fear that if seen and known for who we really are, we will no longer be wanted. In the DVD, Sue said, "They're not gonna want me for who I am so what can I do to make them need me?"

10. Invite a few women to try to put their deepest fear into words. Then point out to the women that we have this in common with one another. If it is easy to see that a fear in someone else as "not really a possibility," perhaps they can begin to see that it is not going to happen to them either.

WRAP-UP

The good news is that as much as we try to arrange for a good life and *protect ourselves* from pain, our sinful strategies will not work. Oh, they may work for a little while but not for long and they never will give us the results we desire. The only safe place for our hearts is in God. God knows why we do the things we do. And he has mercy on us. He understands our deep fear and longs to replace it with his love. (Perfect love casts out fear.) We are together on this journey of redemption. We are on the road.

Read Hebrews 4:14–16 then close your time with prayer asking Jesus to continue to free us from our self-protective and fallen strategies. Invite Jesus to come and heal our places of deep fear where we don't yet know or believe that we are deeply loved and wanted.

You may want to end this session with a quiet song for them to rest in before leaving.

The Wound

THE GOAL

In this lesson we want to honor and give weight to the story and the pain of women's personal histories. We want them to come to know that their lives matter, their hearts matter, what happened to them *matters*.

The purpose of this session is not to whine about our lives but to uncover the wounds and unlock the pain so that we may know further healing. All women are wounded and their wounds are neither too trivial nor too horrendous for God to *heal*.

YOUR INTRODUCTION

Welcome the women back. If you are in a small group setting, check in with each other. "How's your week been?" Set up your time together by admitting that "This week's topic is a tough one. The wound is not an easy thing to talk about." Offer some encouragement right up front along the lines that the purpose of talking about our wounds is not to send us spiraling into a depression or to have a pity party. Rather, the point is to prepare us to experience *deeper healing* from God. As God continues to heal our hearts, it frees us to be more truly able to receive his love and love him in response, with our whole heart.

You may want to choose to show a video clip here. It will help the women access their hearts and prepare them for the DVD. There are several great ones out there to choose from. You will want to set up the clip by giving a little background information that leads up to the scene they are about to watch. (They don't need to know the whole movie—they just need the barest possible background information.) The scene in the movie *The Secret of the Traveling Pants* (Scene 28) where Carmen confronts her father over the phone is a very good one. Many women receive wounding from their father, either from his abuse or his absence. This scene may make lots of women cry. I do. After you show it, react to it.

Then transition by reading Isaiah 61:1–3 reminding the women why Jesus came—to heal our broken hearts and to set *free* the places that are captive within us.

If you want to play a song, "Resurrection" by Nicol Sponberg (*Resurrection* CD) is excellent.

WATCH THE VIDEO

QUIET REFLECTION

Invite the women to journal a few minutes about what they've just watched or about a memory that came to them while watching the DVD. Play something soft in the background. *Adagio* is perfect here.

BREAK

SHARE; HEART TO HEART

1. Begin by reading Psalm 109:21–22.
2. It's time to invite the women to share a part of their story. Remind them of the confidentiality here and that you know it can be hard but that you are in it together. You also want to say something about respecting each other's stories by listening to each other well and not offering advice or trying to fix or diminish someone's wound. Say something like, "Everyone has a story to tell. Just like their hearts, their story *matters*." Have tissues available.
3. You should go first to set the example. You can't share everything but you can share some things. Tell two or three stories from your childhood that you remember had a role in shaping you. You'll want to take about ten to twelve minutes. (I know this

is hugely abbreviated. If a woman was able to tell her whole story, she would need two to three hours.)

4. Then invite someone to go next. "Who's ready to tell us about their wound?" Let the women volunteer rather than calling on someone. There may be a long pause here before someone offers. Normally, just sharing their stories will take your entire discussion time. Depending on how many women you have and how it flows, you may actually need two weeks for this.

5. A woman may have difficulty accessing her heart and may tell her story in the third person. That's okay. It's also okay to ask her a question or two. Another woman may deeply access her pain and begin to sob. That's okay too. Come alongside and gently touch her hand or arm. Let her cry. Tears are good. If she begins to break down heavily, tell her that her tears are good. Let her weep. Ask a couple of women to pray for her. Let it subside and then move on with some gentle encouragement like, "Thank you, Betty. This is not the end of your story. We're on a journey and we talk about our wounds so that God can heal them. He will come."

6. There are times when a woman says she doesn't remember any wounding. She had a marvelous childhood and the parents we all long for. She may have another wound she'd like to talk about from an older age. That's fine. Have her share that story.

7. If the women are having a hard time identifying their wound, take another direction. Ask, "What was your relationship with your father like while you were growing up? What did you do together? What about with your mom?"

8. If every woman tells a piece of her story and there is time left, ask, What was the message to you in answer to your question, *"Am I lovely? Do you delight in me?"* The message to Lori, Leigh, and Stasi was, "No. You aren't. You aren't wanted." To Sue, the message was that "if I come up with *something* other than myself then maybe I'll be loved." To Julie, the message was, "You are alone, not wanted, and life is up to you."

IF YOU NEED MORE TIME

Listening to the stories of each other's wounds is a *crucial* part of this journey. Don't rush through it. You may very well need another week. Take it. Devote next week to the wound. Tell the women who have not shared yet that you are looking forward to hearing from them next week. If you don't need or aren't able to take another week, tell the women that next week we're moving into receiving deeper healing from God. Remind the group to begin work on the next lesson by reading the appropriate chapters and taking their time with the study guide.

WRAP-UP

Your wrap-up is crucial. Don't try to quickly sweep this under the rug or offer platitudes about "all things work together for good." Yes, in Christ, they do. But for now, acknowledge how hard it is to go into the wound and thank them for their honesty. Make it clear that:

+ Every woman carries a wound.

+ The wound nearly always comes from the father, or the lack of one.

+ The wound strikes at the core of our femininity, at our deepest question, "Am I lovely? Do you delight in me?" and answers no.

+ We need to experience deeper and ongoing healing of our wounded hearts in order to live the life God has for us, receive his love and love him in return.

Remind them that as the Scriptures say, *"weeping may last for the night, but a shout of joy comes in the morning."* (Psalm 30:5 NASB). Tell them your plan for next week. Pray.

Healing the Wound

THE GOAL

The goal of this lesson is for the women to give Jesus access to their hearts in an increased and deeper way, so that He might heal them. Hoorah! Women will be coming to this session from a wide spectrum. Some will have done a lot of previous "work" in their hearts processing pain, experiencing healing. For others, it will be brand new, their pain fresh, and for some overwhelming.

Your role is to offer them hope and help usher them to Jesus Christ so that he heal them.

Healing is an ongoing process. We continue in it. We walk in it. There is no one prayer that leaves us completely healed. Substantial healing is available on this side of Heaven. The gospel is all about our restoration as women. Perfect healing comes on the other side. But there is more healing available, for all of us, *now*.

Some women may get stuck seeking after understanding—Why did it happen? Why did I react the way I did? Understanding is lovely, but it is not the same thing as healing.

The goal is *healing*.

YOUR INTRODUCTION

Welcome the women back. Some of them may have had a pretty hard week; opening up the wound may have left them feeling raw, tender, and vulnerable. Ask them how they are. A few may have stories to tell of how God has come for them in new ways bringing them healing. Invite them to take a few minutes to share their stories; they will be encouraging to the other women as well.

Read Isaiah 61—the core of Jesus' mission:

> *The Spirit of the Sovereign Lord is on me,*
> *because the LORD has anointed me*
> *to preach good news to the poor.*
> *He has sent me to bind up the brokenhearted,*
> *to proclaim freedom for the captives*
> *and release from darkness for the prisoners. (v.1)*

A powerful scene to show is from *Les Miserables* (scene 11) when Jean Val Jean intervenes on Fontine's behalf. He comes between her and Javier, the police commissioner who symbolizes the law. This clip is about eight minutes long and worth every second.

After you show the scene, react to it. Tell the women that Val Jean is a picture of Christ coming for them, intervening *for them*. The law says they are guilty. God says, in Christ, they are innocent. Fontine sees herself as nothing but a whore—defined by her wounds and the story of her life. Val Jean says, no . . . she is an innocent and beautiful woman. It's time for God to tell us the truth about who we are in the places in our hearts where we have believed the messages that came with our wounds.

WATCH THE VIDEO

QUIET REFLECTION

Invite the women to take a couple of minutes to quietly journal.

BREAK

SHARE; HEART TO HEART

Begin your time together by having the women turn to Page 95 in *Captivating*. Begin by reading Isaiah 61 in the more familiar words and then the whole page.

1. Start your discussion by saying that what you are after during this time together is healing. The way that God heals our hearts is deeply personal. For one woman, it may happen in a dramatic moment; for another, it takes place over time. Even after we've experienced some deep healing, God will often take us back again, a year or two later for a deeper work of healing.

2. Have they been able to identify the message that came with their wounds? It would be good to have them share those (either for the first time or by way of reminder).

3. Are they able to put into words what they have been wounded into believing about themselves?

4. How have they been mishandling their hearts? (What have they been doing with their pain? Oftentimes the answer is heaping more contempt upon it.) Has it been working?

5. Tell them, "We all still have questions. Am I lovely? Do you delight in me? Am I captivating? God, our True Father, longs to answer that for us, personally, intimately. What would you love for his answer to you to be?" Share your answer first. (You will want to write down what every woman says here as well. It is a deep clue into what is most true for each of them.)

6. Now, for the best part. Spend the rest of your time together praying through the steps to healing. These are steps, a path, a way to walk in, and to live. Ask them if they are willing and ready to give Jesus access and invite deeper healing? That's why we're here. You will want to pray slowly and give plenty of pauses for the words to sink in and for the women to make it personal. Don't rush through this.

Say something like, "I think it would be good for us to take Jesus up on his offer! What we're going to do now is pray together. I am going to pray out loud, and I want you to follow along with me in your hearts, agreeing. I will be pausing in several places for you to make it personal. . . I know this is deeply personal. It's also so beautiful. Let's go to God together. Let's ask him!"

"It begins with surrender. We give ourselves fully over to God."

To enter the journey towards the healing of your feminine heart, all it requires is a "Yes. OK." A simple turning in the heart. Like the prodigal son, we wake one day to see that the life we've constructed is no life at all. We let desire speak to us again, we let our heart have a voice.

(Captivating)

Dear God, this isn't working. My life is a disaster. Jesus—I'm sorry. Forgive me. Please come for me

> *Jesus, I belong to you. You have ransomed me with your very life. I give you my body as a living sacrifice. I give you my soul and my spirit as well. I give you my will, my words and my deeds. I give you my mind and my heart. I give my whole self back to you—all those parts of me that I like and all those I am ashamed of. I give you my past, my present and my future. I surrender all that I am or have been or long to be to you, Jesus. I am yours. Amen.*

Give him permission. Give him access to your broken heart. Ask him to come to *these* places.

> *Yes, Jesus, yes. I do invite you in. Come to my heart in these shattered places.* (You know what they are—ask him there. Is it the abuse? The loss of your father? The jealousy of your mother? Ask him in). *Come to me, my Savior. I open this door of my heart. I give you permission to heal my wounds. Come to me here. Come for me here.*

Renounce the agreements you've made.

> *Jesus, forgive me for embracing these lies. This is not what you have said of me. You said I am your daughter, your beloved, your cherished one. I renounce the agreements I made with* (Name the specific messages you've been living with. "I'm stupid. I'm ugly." You know what they are). *I renounce the agreements I've been making with these messages all these years. Bring the truth here, O Spirit of Truth. I reject these lies.*

Forgive.

Okay—now for a hard step (as if the others have been easy). A real step of courage and will. We must forgive those who hurt us. The reason is simple. Bitterness and unforgiveness are claws that set their hooks deep in our hearts; they are chains that keep us held captive to the wounds and the messages of those wounds. Until you forgive, you remain their prisoner. Paul warns us that unforgiveness and bitterness can wreck our lives and the lives of others (Ephesians 4:31; Hebrews 12:15). We have to let them go.

Forgive as Christ has forgiven you. (Colossians 3:13)

> *My dear Jesus, thank you for forgiving me all my sins at the cross. Please help me to forgive others as well. It's hard, Lord. But you do it. Would you please*

forgive them through me? Jesus, by your grace, with your strength and in your
Name, I forgive _____ for _____. I release them to
you. I lay them down at your feet. I bring your cross and your blood between
us. Please cleanse me of my sin again, and cleanse me of theirs. Forever. In Jesus'
name, I pray. Amen.

Ask Jesus to heal.

We turn from our self-redemptive strategies. We open the door of our hurting heart to Jesus. We renounce the agreements we made with the messages of our wounds, renounce any vows we made. We forgive those who harmed us. And then, with an open heart, we simply ask Jesus to heal us. "He likes to be asked" (C.S. Lewis, *The Magician's Nephew).*

> *Dear Jesus, come to me and heal my heart. Come to the shattered places*
> *within me. Come for the little girl that was wounded. Come and hold me in*
> *your arms, and heal me. Do for me what you promised to do—heal my broken*
> *heart and set me free. Amen.*

Ask him to destroy your enemies.

> *Jesus, come and rescue me. Set me free from (you know what you need free-*
> *dom from). Release me from darkness. I reject them and ask you to destroy them.*
> *Set me free. Amen.*

Receive his love.

> *Father, I need your love. Come to the core of my heart. Come and bring*
> *your love for me. Help me to know you for who you really are—not as I see my*
> *father. Reveal yourself to me. Reveal your love for me. Tell me what I mean to*
> *you. Come and father me. Amen.*

Ask him to answer your question.

Finally, we ask God to bestow our identity. He is our True Father. We bring our heart's question to *him.*

And Father, now I want to ask you, "What do you think of me as a woman? Do you
delight in me? Am I captivating to you?"

You may want to play a song here while the women rest and wait on God. Darrell

Evans' *"Father, My Home is You"* or Mercy Me's *"Word of God Speak"* are two good choices. You want something soft and quiet.

7. Close your time by reading Isaiah 62:3, 4. It is our promise from him.

8 This is just the beginning. God will come and he does heal, and we grow in letting him. We need God to father us. We are his children, his daughters, his beloved ones. Stay with the question. Continue asking him how he sees you. The hard part will be believing that what he says is true! Because when you do hear what he truly feels about you, it will be so close to what you have always wanted, you'll think you are making it up! You aren't. Let it be true.

WRAP-UP

Encourage the women to stay with the question until they get an answer. It may have come when you prayed. It may come on their drive home. It may not come in a way they can receive it for months. But stay. Wait. Look to God. His words to them (to us) can come in surprising ways! Yes, through a Scripture that leaps off the page to you. Or book, a song on the radio, a line in a movie. Try to get away to be alone with God this week for at least an hour. Go for a walk, or just sit. Ask him to speak to you.

Pray.

Spiritual Warfare

THE GOAL

The goal of this lesson is twofold—to "demystify" spiritual warfare as some scary, odd thing and to ignite women to rise up. In the Western church, spiritual warfare has often been treated oddly, either receiving way too much focus (this is rare) or none at all (this is widespread). We want women to learn that being under spiritual attack is a *normal* part of every Christian's life—especially Christians who are growing in Christ! And, we want them to grow in knowing how to battle effectively, *in* Christ, for themselves and for others.

YOUR INTRODUCTION

Welcome the women back. Introduce today's topic of spiritual warfare by saying that it has been good to begin to learn and hear their stories from one another. And each story, like every story we love, has a villain, a bad guy. There is an enemy and we are called to resist him.

They don't need to fear spiritual warfare. The whole point of spiritual warfare is to free us to *love Jesus more*. Jesus remains front and center and is our focus! Tell the women that we are *not* teaching that every hard aspect of their life is the result of spiritual warfare. There are still our wounds that need deeper healing, relational issues that need addressing, and physical illness remains a reality. We are not living in Eden any longer, and we are not Home yet either! However, spiritual warfare makes everything *worse.* Remind them of the second part of Isaiah 61—that Jesus came to set the captives *free.* In order to be free to love Jesus and help others be free to love Jesus, we must obey the Scriptures and stand firm against the evil one.

The clip from the movie, *The Lord of the Rings: The Return of the King* (scene 41: 2:12:10) where Eowyn slays the evil wraith is also a good one. Also from the same movie but earlier (Scene 16 53:52—55:41) where Eowyn stops listening to the lies of Wormtongue, says his words are poison, and walks out into the free air is a good one. If you use this one, point out that the creepy man is trying to get Eowyn to agree with him about her life. (Saying her brother abandoned her. No he didn't! Saying she's all alone. No she isn't!) Victory comes when she won't do it.

A good song to play is "Steel Bars" by Jill Phillips. You could use it at the beginning or at the end in the small groups.

WATCH THE VIDEO

QUIET REFLECTION

BREAK

SHARE; HEART TO HEART

1. Welcome the women back. How was their week? Ask if this category, spiritual warfare, is a new one for them to think on. Does it make them nervous, uncomfortable . . . what?

2. Ask the women what it's been like doing this study together so far. What have they been feeling or "hearing" about their participation in the group? In the video, the women share that they have come under accusation that they are talking too much, talking too little, don't fit in, never will. Any of that sound familiar? Sometimes hearing the whispers that are coming against other women's hearts gives room for women to consider that the whispers *they* are hearing may not be true either. If you want to go further, ask them what they hear or feel when they pass a mirror.

3. In the DVD, Leigh shares the story of God revealing that her battle with her skin came directly from the enemy. She said she couldn't understand why. "Why me?" Then she realized that she was right in the middle of two kingdoms colliding and that Satan wants to destroy what God loves most. That would be us, his beloved!

4. Are they ready to believe that they personally have an enemy? If there is no enemy then everything is either God's fault or their own. (As in, I'm blowing it and God's holding out on me.) What if there is another character on the scene?

5. Read 1 Peter 5:8 and 9. Talk together about spiritual warfare being a *normal* part of every Christian's life and that God calls us to *resist*. We want to learn what it means to resist and get better at it!

6. What in their life may be warfare or made worse by warfare that they hadn't considered before?

7. Have the women share how they would describe the "theme" of warfare that has come against them.

8. Scripture is essential here. Assign these Scriptures to women who have their Bibles and take turns reading them one after the other.

   + Colossians 2:15

   + 1 John 4:4

   + Colossians 1:13–14

   + Romans 8:15

   + James 4:7

   + Ephesians 6:10–18

   + John 10:10

9. In the book, we talk about Satan having a "special hatred" for women because they are beautiful and Satan fell because of his pride in his beauty. He can never be beautiful again. Women are life givers. We bring life and his is a kingdom of death. Have the women respond to this.

WRAP-UP

Jesus came that we might have life and life to the full. In order to have the life God wants for you, you must rise up and take your stand in him. There is a fierceness that

God placed in women and *this* is what it is for. Men aren't our enemy. People are not the enemy. But you have one. There is no reason to fear him, but you must not close your eyes, plug your ears and hope he just goes away. He won't. *You* must **Resist!**

Close in prayer! Practice! Take a stand against the enemy in the name of Jesus Christ, out loud. Have the women pray to bring the cross of Christ and the blood of Jesus to bear against all spirits of (whatever has been previously named—accusation, shame, depression), and send it to the throne of Jesus Christ for judgment. Announce that you belong to God and greater is He that is in you than he that is in the world. Ask God to continue teaching you and strengthening you to stand firm against the devil. In Jesus' name!

LESSON SIX

Romanced

THE GOAL

The goal of this lesson is to more deeply awaken the women to the ways that Jesus has and is romancing them. We want them to grasp that God is not after their performance but after their hearts. Yes, he loves obedience, but only when it flows from a heart that *loves* him.

We want the women to come to know that they are loved right now, today, in this moment. God is not waiting to love them until they reach a certain level of performance. He is smitten with them and longs for them to love him and receive his love.

YOUR INTRODUCTION

Welcome the women back and begin your time by showing them a scene from *Shall We Dance?* (Scene 15) which culminates in the lead character, played by Richard Gere, coming up the escalator, dressed the nines carrying a red rose. The scene ends with him dancing with his wife. Don't set it up. Just show it. (Another great scene is the one we mention in the DVD from *Pride and Prejudice* or the trailer from the movie!)

Come back up and react to the clip. Perhaps just a deep sigh is needed. As women we often long to be romanced; to be fought for, to be pursued, wooed, and won. It is an ageless longing and one that remains no matter our marital status.

Read Isaiah 62:1–5. Tell the women that God is the Author of romance. He is the Ageless Romancer; that Christianity is in fact an invitation to a life of romance with him; a life of intimacy, beauty and adventure.

WATCH THE VIDEO

QUIET REFLECTION

BREAK

SHARE; HEART TO HEART

1. Begin your time together by remembering your favorite movies and stories and who it is they you want to be. In the DVD, I shared that as a young girl I wanted to be Audra Barkley from *The Big Valley*, Lori wanted to be Hayley Mills, Julie wanted to be Anne in *Anne of Green Gables*. Who did they want to be? Who do they want to be now?

2. Flesh out the desire to be romanced. It involves pursuit, being wanted, known. It involves intimacy.

3. Have these desires been substantially met? (Usually the answer is no. Touched? I hope so. But there is still hope because God longs to bring this to us himself, and he is the very best at it!)

4. When you first became a Christian, what did you think God wanted from you? For most of us, we quickly came to believe that what God wanted from us was our service, our work, our duty. We tried really hard to measure up at least on the outside. Most of us believed the level of our godliness was measured by external factors. Let the women tell their stories, then direct them to the reality that what God is after is the heart. As Leigh said in the DVD, "It's your heart that is central. That is where the intimacy is."

5. Read Hosea 2:14, then ask the women what they would love for God to say to them. You lead the way. Yes, this is vulnerable and honest. That's what is needed here.

6. Take a moment and invite the women to consider that it is true. That what they long for Jesus to say to them is exactly what he *is* saying to them.

7. In the DVD, Sue said that God is restoring the pleasure and joys to her that she had growing up in the form of riding a bike. She isn't riding it for exercise but for fun! What would the women like for God to *restore* to them?

8. By now, the women have been bringing their core question to God, "Am I lovely? Do you delight in me?" for a couple of weeks. Have any women heard an answer they are willing to share? Let them.

9. Remember that one of the key ways that God heals our heart is in answering our question. Encourage the women to stay with the question. Even if they've heard from God, they need to keep believing, keep going to him.

10. Since we've talked about the romance a little and how personal it is, have those who can share stories of how the romance came to them when they were young and how is it coming to them these days?

11. This is also where we briefly introduce worship as a way of offering our hearts to Jesus and cultivating intimacy with him. Read Matthew 22:37 and ask the women what is it that God most wants from them? The answer is their love.

WRAP-UP

God is not after servants who love, but *lovers* who serve. Encourage the women to keep their eyes and *the eyes of their hearts* open so that they might see and recognize the ways that Jesus is coming for them now. This week. Today.

Close your time by worshipping together and giving the women the opportunity to practice bringing the adoration of their hearts to God. Play one song like "I Am Yours" from Darrell Evans's *Let the River Flow* CD or "Beautiful One" from By The Tree's *Hold You High* CD.

Afterwards, pray, telling God how absolutely marvelous he is and also asking him to bring his romancing of us in a way we quickly recognize it as from him. Pray for the women to have eyes to see and hearts to receive the personal, intimate love of God.

(Another great song is "When You Say You Love Me" by Josh Groban. This song is more about God singing to us than us singing to God.)

Loving a Man

THE GOAL

The goal of this lesson is for the women to have their eyes opened to what fuels a man, what *he* desires. Women play a crucial role in the lives of men, not only their husbands, but also their brothers, sons, friends, bosses and coworkers. We want to pull back the curtain on a man's heart to enable a woman to play her role more powerfully and with godly intention.

As a side note, we just began to scratch the surface on this topic in the DVD. This could well be a study in itself! But hopefully, it will be enough to get the women thinking!

YOUR INTRODUCTION

Welcome the women back and begin your time by introducing the topic, "Loving a Man." Whether we are married or not, we all have men in our lives. And we all can grow in relating to them better, understanding them more, and calling them out more effectively to be the men they are meant to be.

This session is for married women, but it is for single women too. As women, we want to call forth the true masculinity in all the key men in our lives, not just the ones we are married to.

Men have a question too. It's a little different than ours but just as deep. It goes something like, "Do I have what it takes? Am I a real man?" The best thing a woman can do is answer his question with a *yes* in every possible way—with her words and her actions. Many wives are telling their husbands just the opposite and it is crippling them. Men long to be delighted in as well; it fuels their actions as does the story of their lives.

Ultimately, just like us, men need to bring their question to their Father God to receive deep healing, validation, and have their true identity bestowed. A woman can help point him to God and also affirm him that the "Yes!" answer he longs for is the one he will get. He has what it takes. She sees it.

A fabulous film clip is from the movie "Cinderella Man" (Scene 17, 1:47—1:51). Maye has not been supportive of her husband's big boxing match. She fears for his life. She realizes that by withholding her support, she is giving him a great handicap. She goes to him before the match and tells him she is fully behind him and reminds him who he is. It's a marvelous example of how a woman strengthens a man with her words.

WATCH THE VIDEO

QUIET REFLECTION

BREAK

SHARE; HEART TO HEART

Welcome the women back and check in with each other. How are they? How was it living with the desire to be Romanced more awakened? Did anyone recognize, receive or remember any romancing from God this week? Have them share any stories.

1. It's a little odd to go from the Romance to talk about Loving a Man and say that the romance doesn't revolve around a man. But it's true. We need God and so do they. And yes, we need each other as well. Remind the women of the core questions in a man's heart and ask each about a key man in her life—her father, her husband . . . and how was his question answered in his youth?

2. For those who are married, ask if they know the full story of their husband's life. Does their husband know theirs? Encourage them to take an uninterrupted evening or two and share their stories. This is such a powerful and eye-opening

experience. For the women who are not married, they could share their story with a trusted friend or perhaps with your group if it is small enough and you have the time; it is honoring and redemptive.

3. Although a woman cannot ultimately answer the deep question in a man's heart, what can she do?

4. In the video, the men said that they want to be loved, respected, and trusted. They said that the *best* thing a woman can do to love a man is to love herself and make Jesus a priority. For me personally, coming to rest in the love of God more deeply freed me to love John and take risks with him in sharing my heart honestly and vulnerably because I knew I was safe in Jesus. Our marriage grew and changed so much because I was much less afraid of John's response. Have the women respond to the men's statement.

5. Read Ephesians 5:1. What does living a life of love mean to you regarding your relationships with men? The answers you want to direct them toward are not hiding, offering their beauty, strength, and vulnerability. We will flesh out our "beauty" more later but when we speak of it, we are speaking of their inner beauty, their unique gifting, the way they see, and the beauty of their lives, form, and face. The smile of a woman is a great balm to a weary soul.

6. How do men *not* want to be treated by women? OK, this is a pretty easy one. They don't want to be nagged. They don't want to be mothered. They don't want to be treated as incompetent. This one will require further repentance for all of us. And cunning.

7. Not all the men in these women's lives are good men. Some are actually really bad. The way you love a good man is different from how you would love a wicked man. I'd recommend Dan Allender's book *Bold Love*. Maybe get it yourself. At the back it has godly wisdom on how to love all kinds of men. You may want to talk a little bit here about their vulnerability. When we say for women to offer their vulnerability, we mean to offer it wisely and not to *everyone*. We need to walk with God, live in godly counsel and grow in our relationship with Christ, knowing his love.

8. Can a man truly answer the core question in a woman's heart?

9. Read 1 Peter 3:6. How does this relate to living a life of love? The fear of man is a snare. If we fear, we won't offer our true hearts. We won't offer at all. God tells us not to fear them!

WRAP-UP

Alluring Adam to the heart of God can be done by women in countless ways. It can be done without a word. God wants us to encourage one another, to love each other into becoming the man or woman that he created us to be. Women lead and love by the example of their lives; primarily by growing in relationship with Christ.

Close your time with prayer. Pray something like:

Father, we give you our lives and hearts and desires and longings. Please continue to heal us, romance us, and reveal your love to us. Open our eyes to your intimate romancing and continue answering our question. Help us to love the men in our lives in the way you want us to. Thank you, Jesus, that you know we are still afraid and you know why. We ask for your mercy and grace. Reveal to us the places you are working in us that we need to repent and to change. Come, reveal to us how deeply you love us and how safe we are in you. Help us to become the woman we long to be. We love you, Jesus. And it's in your Name that we pray. Amen.

Beauty to Unveil

THE GOAL

The goal of this lesson is to broaden the definition of beauty in the minds of the women. *Beauty is the external expression of an inward reality.* It is what we do, what we say, what we offer and how we look. Beauty flows from an awakened heart in love with Jesus. The more his we become, the more beautiful we become!

I have yet to meet a woman under fifty years old who is comfortable with her beauty and believes she is lovely. And I have only met a few over fifty! It takes a while! The messages of our wounds, the story of our lives, the accusations of the enemy, and the advertising from Madison Avenue all tell us that we are not beautiful.

But God (two of my favorite words in the Bible) *says we are beautiful.* Right now. To him. He says our beauty flows from our hearts. And he is captivated by us. For the women to consider this as the deeper reality is the goal.

YOUR INTRODUCTION

Welcome the women! You might share the goal of this lesson as part of your introduction. Say that you know beauty is difficult to talk about. It's messy and hard and painful and even more difficult to define.

But we are women. Made in the image of God. And God is altogether *beautiful.*

Walking around believing that we are ugly and have nothing to offer doesn't do him, or us, or anyone else any good. God wants us to *know* we are lovely and rest in it. He invites us to look to him, to his heart as our first and most important mirror.

He says, "How beautiful you are, my darling! Oh, how beautiful!" (Song of Solomon 4:1)

WATCH THE VIDEO

QUIET REFLECTION

As always, play something soft and lovely while the women journal their reactions for a few minutes.

BREAK

SHARE; HEART TO HEART

1. We are made in the image of God and one of the core ways we bear his image is in our beauty. It is the essence of femininity. Beauty invites, nourishes, protects, inspires, comforts, strengthens, and speaks to the world that *all is well.* Ask the women who is or has been beautiful to them? Invite the women to share stories from their lives, the Bible, or historical women. Let this go on for a while. Hopefully, through their stories, you will be able to help flesh out the broader, truer definition of beauty.

2. Leigh shared about Corrie ten Boom's sister, Betsy, who told her sister that "there is no pit so deep that God is not deeper still." She helped her sister to love against all the forces of darkness and bring that message to the world. Is there a woman who has dramatically impacted your heart, your life for God? Who? How? Tell stories, then point out how utterly beautiful that is.

3. Read 1 Peter 3:3–5. What is the "unfading beauty of a gentle and quiet spirit"? (Faith. Increasingly growing in loving and trusting God by faith!)

4. Are the women beginning to understand that when we speak about beauty being the essence of femininity that we are not talking about their outward appearance? Does it help to draw the parallel between the essence of men being strength—and we are not talking about big muscles but about a quality of soul?

5. Do they believe they are beautiful? Have an inward beauty to offer? (If the women

know each other well, this is a wonderful opportunity to take some time and offer words of encouragement to each other. Share stories of how they are and have been beautiful.)

6. You might want to pray at this point. From the study guide:

> *Dear God, You are beautiful and I believe I bear your image. But you know that I don't feel very pretty let alone beautiful. Would you please come to this place in my heart . . . this core place . . . and reveal to me my own beauty? Please heal the places in my heart that have been assaulted and hurt regarding beauty. And establish your truth here. Do you think I'm beautiful? How? Why? Please help me, Jesus. It's in your name that I pray. Amen.*

7. In the DVD, Lori shared that she is beginning to get glimpses of her beauty that she's always had but didn't believe she had through the love of God. She is growing in truly knowing that God loves her and as she says, 'If he can delight in me, then I know something's there."

   Read Psalm 45:11. The King is enthralled by your beauty. Enthralled means captured or captivated by. Take a moment and ask God to make this truth come deeper within all your hearts.

8. Believing that we have no real beauty of our own to offer that would be *wanted* keeps us from offering. We hide. The women in the video shared what it would look like for them to stop hiding in areas where they are aware they continue to hide. What would it look like for the women in your group? (Risk talking, offering, calling someone, volunteering, inviting, being known?)

9. The key to being able to offer our beauty lies in 1 Peter 3:6. Do not give way to fear. What are the women afraid of?

10. How has being afraid kept them from offering their true beauty?

11. In the DVD, Leigh mentions the story of Cinderella as being all of our stories. When she watched it as a young girl, she couldn't understand how Cinderella could possibly not know she was lovely. Later, Leigh realized that she, too, was believing the lies of the wicked stepsisters and believing that it was God's voice telling her to "work more," "clean more," "you belong in the basement" and was not the voice of her enemy.

    What about them? Have they felt like Cinderella before the Prince comes?

12. The gospel is a gospel of restoration. Read Isaiah 61:1–3. (Have you memorized

it by now?!) It says that God is bestowing beauty for ashes. He is the one restoring us. He is the one removing our shame and restoring our hearts. He says we are lovely. Do they want to believe him?

WRAP-UP

God is inviting the women to a Sacred Romance. He says they are beautiful. He doesn't want them to work harder, try harder, hide more . . . he wants them to come out of hiding and offer him and their world their true heart. Like Mary of Bethany, he wants us to risk offering and loving him with our whole hearts.

He is making us beautiful. As we look to him, as we grow in him, we are being changed into his likeness. And he is the *most beautiful* person, ever. We don't have to conjure it. We don't have to strive after it. We just have to grow in trusting his heart of love for us. Right now.

We must keep asking Jesus to show us our beauty. Invite the women to pray along with you, and ask Jesus what he thinks of them as women. His words to us let us rest. And unveil our beauty.

Psalm 27:4
> *One thing I ask of the LORD,*
> *this is what I seek:*
> *that I may dwell in the house of the LORD*
> *all the days of my life,*
> *to gaze upon the beauty of the LORD*
> *and to seek him in his temple.*

Irreplaceable Role

THE GOAL

The goal of this lesson is for women to see that they long for an irreplaceable role to play because they have one! God has woven it into our hearts. The way we live it out will look different from woman to woman. We would also love to shed light on the fact that an irreplaceable role in the eyes of God and his Kingdom looks very different from the eyes of the world.

YOUR INTRODUCTION

Welcome the women back. Introduce today's topic of our desire to play an irreplaceable role in a heroic adventure as being key to our hearts. We desire it because God placed the desire within us. It is where we bear his image!

For many women, the creation story has *not* been a source of great personal inspiration. Many of us have felt secondary, inferior, and even rebellious about the creation order. We haven't liked being called a "Helper." But that is because we have not understood its meaning. Women are created as man's *ezer kenegdo*, which is a position of great honor and glory. We want to come to know that more deeply!

Back in the garden, in Genesis 1:28, God gave the mandate to rule and subdue the earth to both men and women. Women are crucial, essential! Irreplaceable.

A great film clip to show is a scene from the movie, *The Lord of the Rings: The Fellowship of the Ring* (Scene 17 through 1:13:21) This is when Arwen comes on the scene and rides with the wounded Frodo across the river into her father's domain with the forces of evil in hot pursuit. Arwen is needed. She is the fastest rider. She is the one who saves not only Frodo, but all Middle-earth as well. She is irreplaceable. (It is also a good picture of a woman turning and facing her enemies and *standing firm*.)

WATCH THE VIDEO

As with all the videos, you may want to edit this to shorten it for your group if you are under time constraints.

QUIET REFLECTION

BREAK

SHARE; HEART TO HEART

1. Welcome the women back and ask them what struck them the most about this chapter. Do they resonate with this desire? Have they understood that being a woman, created as an *ezer*, has such immense dignity and value?
2. Who are their favorite women in the Bible and why? Talk about them and how they played their unique irreplaceable role so well! (Mary of Bethany, Mary the mother of God, Esther, Ruth . . . so many to choose from!)
3. Several women in the video mentioned Mary of Bethany as one of their favorites. Leigh said that Mary "was a place for the Lord to come and know that he was wanted and desired and chosen above all else." Have the women react to that.
4. Read Genesis 1:26. "Let them rule." Adam and Eve are corulers of the earth. Is this a new revelation to them? What do they think about that? Do they feel that they are now?
5. What about present-day heroes. Ask the women who they admire and esteem these days. The chance to talk about this together gives the women the opportunity to flesh out the fact that the way women express their "irreplaceable role" varies greatly. Point out to the women the way that the ones they have shared about (maybe even women within your group) are *life givers*, that they are bringing forth *life* in a myriad of different ways.

6. This can be a difficult subject for women who don't feel they are very important in what they are offering. The place of our desire to be irreplaceable has been wounded and often shamed by the world. For example, stay-at-home moms who feel invisible are actually invaluable! Some women may feel they abandoned their true desire and settled. Some may have no idea what their desires were or are.

Tell the women who are struggling with this that the place of our desires to be irreplaceable is holy ground. The enemy has attacked and assaulted this area where we bear God's image. God has written something personal and deep and true on each one of our hearts. Sometimes the way to know what it is, is to look at how we have been wounded. The lies and the attacks of the enemy come directly against our glory—how we bear God's image.

Also, as Julie mentions in the DVD, some desires are more *mythic* than specific. As a little girl, she wanted to be a nurse. She is not a nurse but sees how she does still want to bring healing to the brokenhearted. Does this resonate with some of them?

And, timing varies. God often asks us to lay our desires at his feet for a time until he has us pick them up again. Maybe we want to sing. We have a great voice. But God hides us for a while, perhaps a long while, singing only to him while he does a deep work in our hearts until he pulls the curtain back for us and invites us to sing for others.

7. As we are increasingly healed and growing in Christ, God restores our desires to us. Some are *re*covered and others are *dis*covered. Is God restoring any desires to the women?

8. Now to transition to the holy ground of bringing forth life. Not all women are mothers, but all women are life givers. We don't all give physical birth to babies, but we are invited by God to give birth to all kinds of things! Facilitator's guides for instance! Invite the women to dream a little. Or to dream a lot! What would they love to give birth to?

9. Leigh tells the story of the comparison between the Academy Awards and meeting the Lord. What did the women think of that analogy? What is their reaction to it?

WRAP-UP

God wants us to live our lives with him. Together in every aspect and every moment. He isn't bored with us. And he wants to restore our hearts and our desires to us. He wants us to know that we are irreplaceable! We are vital. To him and to the world.

All women have an irreplaceable role to play and are called to be life givers. The way we live this out expresses itself in myriad ways throughout our lives. You are a woman. You are a lifegiver. You do have an irreplaceable role to play. We need you. God needs you. Choose him. First. Last. And in between.

Close your time in prayer.

Caring for Your Heart

THE GOAL

The goal of this lesson, our final lesson, is to help the women *remember* and to live out Proverbs 4:23. Women need to care for their hearts and often, we fall last on our own list of priorities. Yet, God says that our hearts are a priority. We want to encourage the women to care for their hearts, to grow in their relationship with Christ and to develop godly, encouraging friendships with other women. We can't do it on our own. We need each other.

YOUR INTRODUCTION

Welcome the women back. This is your last time together. Express to the women your heart about this and what you hope to be true for them. Then begin your time with a short review:

Let's begin our time by remembering together. Remember—that the story of your life is the story of the long and fierce pursuit by the One who loves you most and longs to be your first love, to woo and win you for himself. But it is also the story of the long and sustained assault against your heart by one who knows who you could be and fears you.

All of us are wounded, and Jesus came to *heal* our broken hearts and to set the captives *free*. He bestows beauty on us instead of ashes, gladness for mourning and a garment of praise instead of despair.

He tells us our hearts matter. Remember Proverbs 4:23. Above all else guard your heart for from it flow the wellsprings of life within you!

It is in our hearts that we bear the image of our God, in the desires of our heart. The desires to be romanced, to play an irreplaceable role in a heroic adventure and to have a beauty all our own to unveil are placed there by God. They are telling us the truth about who we truly are and the role that is ours to play.

The journey of life is a wonderful, beautiful, and often excruciatingly painful one. In the demands and pressures that we feel, often the first thing we abandon is caring for our hearts. And that is a dangerous thing to do.

God instructs us to guard our hearts as in *protect* them, *shield* them, *watch over* them, *nurture* them, *care* for them. It is in our heart of hearts that all LIFE flows. It is in our hearts that Jesus makes his home, and it is from our hearts that all love, all creativity, all worthy endeavors flow. It is of the utmost importance to God and therefore, should be to us.

An amazing clip to show is the *extended trailer* from *The Lord of the Rings* trilogy. It lasts about 7 minutes but will help the women to remember everything we've talked about.

WATCH THE VIDEO

QUIET REFLECTION

BREAK

SHARE; HEART TO HEART

1. Welcome them back and ask them, "How has this time together been for you?" Let each woman share. This is important.

2. To be present to God, we have to be present to our own hearts. Proverbs 4:23 is probably memorized by now. Have the women tell you what it says and what it means to them. Ask, "How are you doing that? How are you caring for your heart?" Or, "How do you want to begin caring for your heart?"

   Another way to get to the answer is by asking, "What brings you refreshment?" or "How are you carving out time in your life for God?" Let this dialogue go on for a while. Encourage one another to take the time to care, guard, nourish and protect their hearts.

3. This life we are in is a journey, a journey of redemption and further healing and restoration of our hearts as women. God is pursuing us and he promises in his Word to finish that which he has completed. He also tells us not to forsake getting together. We need each other. We need fellowship. We aren't meant to and can't survive living this life alone. Women are relational to their core. We need people and specifically, we need women friends. How have the friendships of women helped them in the past? (For some women, their friendships with women have only been a source of pain and betrayal. Ask God to come and redeem this area of their lives.)

4. Women help bring forth life in one another—that means they partner with God in helping the women to become who they were created to be through encouragement and love. Leigh pointed out in the video that living our quiet lives unto God—seeking him, longing after him, growing in him—impacts more people than we will ever realize and brings forth life *in them*. People are watching how we live, the choices we make, how we respond and what we truly believe more than we know. But *friendships are opposed*. They have to be fought for. Have friendships come easily to these women?

5. What has come against their friendships? (Accusation and misunderstandings are common.)

6. When they fail a friend, or are failed by a friend, what do they usually tend to do? (Withdraw, hide, isolate, wait for the friend to make the first move?) What would they like to do?

7. In order to grow at becoming a better friend, we have to risk believing that 1) we are wanted, 2) we are enjoyed, and 3) our friend is under just as much warfare as we are. Is there a woman or two with whom you would like to pursue a deeper friendship? How can you do that? What will it require of you?

8. In the DVD, we take a few minutes and offer what we see in each other. We call it speaking into each other's lives. This is a good and powerful thing to do and a wonderful way to end your time together. You know your group and if they would be able to do this or not, but ask God. Follow his lead. If you do this, just take a couple of minutes and invite one or two women to speak into one woman's life about what they *see* or *experience* in her. Let the woman react, then move on to the next woman.

9. One of the most feminine things we can do as women is to *respond* with tender-

ness and faith. Song of Solomon 2:10 says, "My lover (Jesus) spoke and said to me, 'Arise my darling, my beautiful one, and come with me.'" Jesus is inviting us to join him, to follow him, to trust him, and to love him. How would you like to respond to him today?

WRAP-UP

In John 10:10, Jesus says *"The thief comes only to steal and kill and destroy; I have come that they may have life, and have it to the full!"* All movement towards life and wholeness, towards restoration is opposed. Yes. We know that. But we do not fight alone. Jesus has come for us and he is coming still. He is our Bridegroom and our valiant Warrior, truly our Knight in shining armor! He will not get tired and he will not give up until we are fully his and fully healed.

He says we are beautiful to him *now*. Today. And he invites us into a Romance with him—not a life of duty and obligation but a life of intimacy, beauty, and adventure. He asks us to play our irreplaceable role right next to him and to offer the beauty that we possess to him first, then to a hungry and hurting world. We are needed. We are wanted. Our core desires have been telling us the truth.

I suggest that you pray and make room for each woman who is willing to pray as well! Thank God for what he has done and for what he is going to do!

As I indicated in the study guide, I am so proud of all of you for doing this! I know it hasn't been easy at times. But the fruit is so very good. Now, stay with it. Don't just run on to the next Bible study or small group. Let your heart marinate in the truths you've received here. Keep asking God to romance you and to answer your core question, "Am I lovely?" He loves our asking. Go over your notes and study guide. Buy the songs that moved you. Help each other to *remember*. Remember the Lord your God. "Remember the wonders he has done!" (1 Chronicles 16:12a)

"My lover is mine and I am his!" (Song of Solomon 2:16)

GOING DEEPER

For women who would like to stay in this message a while longer, *Captivating: A Guided Journal* is a more in-depth study of the material. It is made for personal use or for use with a few women.

NOTES

NOTES

NOTES

NOTES